MW01108337

"A small thing is a small thing, but a small thing done faithfully can become a great thing."

— Colonel Wilson

 "If you do more than you are paid to do, eventually you'll be paid more for what you do."

— Colonel Wilson

 "Things were created to be used, and people were created to be loved. But most often we love things and use people."

— Colonel Wilson

The Merchant

CONTENTS

CHAPTER 1

Sam Wishes His Mom a Happy Birthday

The mornings were muggy in Natchez along the Mississippi River. From his perch atop the bluff, Sam could see the enormous waterway winding through the Delta Cotton Country from the north. It then weaved south, cutting its way toward New Orleans.

Sam would often come to the bluff and sit. He spent his time watching the river flow by. The bluff had been a favorite spot of his mother's as well. She had often brought Sam and his little sister up to the bluff. First, the three of them would lay out an old quilt. Then they would untie the twine that held the brown paper containing fresh corn and bread moist with butter. They would sit for hours watching the river traffic. The Mississippi casts a spell on you. Its majestic beauty keeps you entranced. Since this was his mother's favorite spot, he felt closest to her here.

Sam couldn't believe they were gone— yellow fever with its cruel blade had cut through the community the previous fall. It took Sam's mom and little sister, Rachael. For a while the grief in Sam's heart was so great he felt it might burst. If not for the support and comfort from Granny and family friend, Colonel Wilson, Sam surely would not have made it through the terrible ordeal.

Sam threw a stone over the bluff into the river. He got to his feet, took one last look at the bouquet of fresh flowers from old lady Crawford's summer garden, and tossed them into the river too. As he watched the flowers float away, tears streamed down his face. He whispered, "Happy birthday Mama, I love you." Sam then turned away and started his short walk to town, where he worked at The Mercantile.

CHAPTER 2

The Great Depression Threatens Sam's Job

Sam enjoyed his job at The Mercantile. Natchez had two large general merchandise stores—Traders and The Mercantile. Two competitive steamboat captains who had competed with each other for the Mississippi freight traffic, and who were more than happy to bring their rivalry to land, founded them. The captains started their stores near the end of the steamboat era and enjoyed their success and prosperity.

Unfortunately, with the start of The Great Depression in 1929, a couple of years before, business had gotten very tough in Natchez.

Although the entire country was plunged into the Depression, the South seemed to be hit the hardest. Any job was scarce—good jobs even more scarce.

It was William Barney's bad luck to have bought The Mercantile from its founder just as the Depression started and, as business for the two stores slowed, competition and rivalry increased. It wasn't just pride at stake for Bill Barney now, it was sheer survival.

Sam arrived with the rest of the workers. He put on his apron and joined the other men gathering along the loading docks.

Materials and supplies were arriving by truck and mule-drawn wagons. Mules often took up the slack because gasoline was both scarce and expensive in the Delta.

Sam hovered around the schedule board to get his daily assignment from Mr. Barney. Mr. Barney, a short stocky man, barked out orders and complained about the tools and equipment left out from the previous day. Slightly overweight, he had a distinct walk about him. It was more of a waddle. Today, his pants, which were too short, revealed mismatched socks that seemed to reveal his personality to anyone who happened to notice as he passed by.

Sam soon found himself busy stocking shelves with his friend and coworker, Dalton. They had been working side by side for a while when Dalton whispered in Sam's ear, "Johnny James heard Mr. Barney talking about things getting slow—much slower than last year. He said this depression is hitting us hard. Know what that means don't you, Sam?"

"No, what's it mean?

"It means that some of us are 'bout to be laid off, that's what it means."

"Who's getting laid off?" asked a concerned Sam.

"Johnny James says probably the youngest and the newest will get the ax first," said Dalton.

Sam felt his heart drop, "That means us."

"You catch on quick," Dalton replied sarcastically.

Sam couldn't speak. He couldn't lose this job, it was all Granny and he had left. Sam worked in silence for most of the day. Dalton tried his best to break through the wall of worry that surrounded his friend but failed.

CHAPTER 3

Sam Learns of the Seeds of Success

When Sam left The Mercantile that evening, he headed to Colonel Wilson's home. Wilson Hall was a huge antebellum mansion built when cotton was king. The massive columns created a picture of elegance, making the old home the envy of Natchez. The mansion had been passed down to Colonel Wilson by his father. The Colonel, a direct descendent of Civil War hero General John T. Wilson, had been a successful cotton gin owner in the Delta. He retired five years ago after his wife of forty years passed away.

The colonel had been a good friend to Sam when he lost his mom and sister. In his spare time, Sam helped keep Wilson Hall in good repair. The Colonel paid him well but didn't need him much this time of year. Sam went straight to the shed and grabbed the clippers. He still had two hours of daylight, so there was no need to waste it. He worked the front part of the 100-year-old hedge that circled the property.

His mind was reeling with thoughts and fears that he might lose his precious job. When darkness forced him to quit, he put the clippers back in the shed and headed toward the back door of the mansion.

He found the Colonel sitting on the rear porch, rocking back and forth, sipping a mint julep. "Son, you look like someone done licked all the red off your candy. Sit and tell me about it," said the Colonel. They sat in silence for a moment. The Colonel asked again, "What's on your mind?"

"I think I'm going to lose my job," said Sam. He then explained his situation at The Mercantile.

The Colonel sat back and lit his pipe. Pondering Sam's predicament for a moment, he said, "Considering how scarce jobs are now, I think you only have one option."

"What's that sir?" asked Sam.

"Well, you need to make yourself too valuable to lose."

"How am I supposed to do that?" asked Sam.

"By learning and planting some Seeds of Success," the Colonel said in his matter-of-fact way.

"Seeds of success?" asked Sam. "What are they?"

"When I ran my cotton gins here in the Delta, they were the most profitable gins in the country. Their success was largely due to the practice by all my people of what I call the 'Seeds of Success.' "

"Well, what are these Seeds of Success Colonel?" said Sam.

The Colonel looked at Sam as if he were trying to make up his mind about something. "Sam, there's an ancient law that is as old as time itself. It says that 'You reap what you sow.' It is upon this law that the Seeds of

Success are based. These Seeds work like you can't imagine. They represent an investment of time and self, but they can make you one of the most valuable workers at whatever job you have.

"The application of these Seeds is contrary to what most folks are taught. But, if you apply these Seeds to your life, you will not only save your job, but you will also become one of the most valuable workers at The Mercantile."

Save his job? Now the Colonel had Sam's attention. "What are these Seeds?"

"Not so fast," said the Colonel solemnly. Since these Seeds go against what most people believe and do, if you are going to be successful with them, they need your total commitment."

Sam respected the Colonel. He didn't think the old man would lead him astray, but he wondered just what "total commitment" would mean. He felt he was already totally committed to supporting himself and Granny, and with the worry about losing his job, he wondered if he had the time or energy to commit to some *seeds* that he was uncertain would help him. His doubt must have showed.

The Colonel reached over and put a big hand on Sam's shoulder. "Have I ever given you reason to doubt me, son?" Sam looked down at his feet, then up into the Colonel's soft, trusting eyes.

"No, sir, you haven't. You've done the exact opposite. You've always been there for me," said Sam.

"Then trust me on this, Sam," said the Colonel.

Sam hesitated for a moment, then nodded, "Okay, I will."

The Colonel smiled and started rocking back and forth. "We'll go through one Seed a week. At the end of each day you'll come and tell me how you applied the particular Seed that day. If, at the end of the week, I feel you have that Seed down pat, we'll proceed on to the next one. Is that okay with you?"

"Well, sir, I really don't have that much time. Why don't you just tell me all five Seeds now?"

"It doesn't work like that. What you'll be doing is developing good habits and building character. These two things are the foundation to all success, but they take time to absorb, to make them a part of who you are. This can't be done in an instant."

The Colonel paused for a minute, his eyes on the young man's face. " You said you trusted me."

"Yes, sir, I do."

Sam paused, then reached out his hand. "I'll do whatever you say Colonel."

The Colonel took his hand and shook it. "I don't think you will be disappointed, Sam."

"I believe the principles these Seeds provide are some of the most valuable advice one can obtain. They represent knowledge that can transform anyone into a successful person. Are you ready to start?"

"Yes sir," said a now excited Sam.

"Seed Number One, 'Excel first, reap later.' "

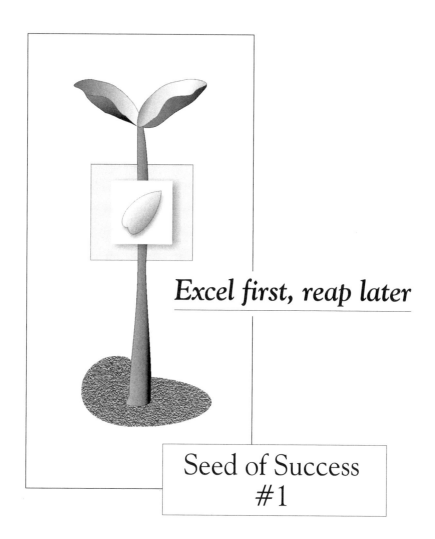

Excel first, reap later

Seed of Success
#1

"I don't understand," said Sam.

"Most people don't. A good many decide that if they get that raise or that promotion then that's when they'll do more. On the other hand, managers quickly discover that people rarely step up the pace or increase productivity when paid to. Oh, sure, their improvement lasts for a short while, but then most people go back to their previous level.

"True winners, Sam, use this to stand out from the crowd. They excel in advance, stepping up their productivity on their own without promises of a raise, promotion, or any other reward. If you do more than you are paid to do, Sam, eventually you'll be paid more for what you do. Always do what is expected of you and then a little extra.

"Think about it this way. Imagine you are a worker at Smith's Bakery. Mr. Smith has hired you to make pies for his bakery. He will pay you twenty-five cents an hour as long as you make five pies in that hour. All his workers start out at the same rate. At this point everything is equal. You get twenty-five cents an hour and Mr. Smith gets five pies made. If you want to make more money, you need to do a little extra work. Now, you can do this in two different ways. Either you make more pies in an hour, or you make a better pie that can be sold for more money. Either way, your doing something extra will be noticed by Mr. Smith."

"Yes, sir, I understand what you mean. What I'm saying is that I'm happy with my twenty-five cents for making five pies. My concern is that I will lose my job making any pies."

"If that's the case, Sam, you still need to do more than what is expected of you. That will set you apart from the rest of the workers, and, unless everyone is laid off, you'll keep your job," said the Colonel.

"How do I do that?" asked Sam.

The Colonel sat back and thought for a moment. "Well, one great way to stand out is to look around and see what needs to be done and take care of it without being asked.

"You see, Sam, managers spend a lot of their time putting out fires and solving problems. Sometimes things that should be addressed, don't get addressed because the manager lacks the time or energy.

"Now, the owner of The Mercantile is Bill Barney. Tell me, Sam, what is it that's bothering Mr. Barney that he hasn't had a chance to take care of?"

Sam gave this some thought. "Well, he sure gripes about people leaving their tools and aprons laying about when they go home."

"Good. Take care of it for him," said the Colonel.

Sam looked at him and grinned, "I think I can do that."

"Okay, every time I see you this next week I'm going to ask you what it is you are doing that is above and beyond your responsibilities at work, something that will increase your value. Your goal is to become so valuable that Mr. Barney cannot afford to lose you."

On his way home, Sam gave considerable thought to how he was going to use first Seed at work the very next day.

CHAPTER 4

Sam Plants the First
Seed of Success

Business was surprisingly good at The Mercantile the next day. Sam kept busy and made an extra effort to do all that was asked of him and a little bit more. As the day ended, Sam's fellow workers left in their usual hurry. Sam looked around and saw what Mr. Barney was facing—aprons and tools were strung about on barrels and crates. Sam gathered all the discarded aprons and headed to the storage room.

As he turned the corner, he ran into Mr. Barney coming from the other direction. "You still here, Sam?" asked Mr. Barney.

"Yes, sir, just picking up a bit before I go."

"I see," said Mr. Barney. Sam then picked up the tools left lying around and headed out the back and down the worn cement stairs to the tool shed.

He heard someone call his name. Sam turned and saw Mr. Barney standing on the loading dock. "Thank you, Sam," he said.

"You're welcome, sir." Sam thought he saw the hint of a smile as Mr. Barney turned and walked back inside.

Later Sam replayed his day with the Colonel. The Colonel smiled and rocked back in forth in his favorite rocker. "You did well today. Just remember, 'Excel first, reap later.' Now go see your Granny. I'm sure she has your supper ready."

Supper was hot on the stove just as the Colonel predicted. Granny and Sam lived in a small, rectangular house with worn wooden siding. Sam had lived here his entire life. It was an old, run-down sharecropper's house that was cold in the winter and hot in the summer. It wasn't much, but it was the only home Sam had ever known. Since the loss of his mother and sister there was a silence about the house.

Sam sat at the small wooden table and ate his greens and cornbread. He knew Granny would have eaten earlier, as was her practice, so she could work in her garden before it got dark.

After finishing his meal, he found Granny out back working in the garden. She was happy to see him.

Granny's garden was famous around Natchez. It was a simple patch in the backyard, but it had the best tasting vegetables in town. Sam walked up and put his arm around her frail little body. He gave her a gentle hug. "Need any help?" he asked. Granny gave him a hug back and said, "Don't reckon so. Light's about played out. Why don't you go inside and brew us up some chicory coffee? Then you can tell me about your day."

As Sam shared his day with Granny, she listened in silence and rocked in her creaky oak rocking chair. When Sam was done, Granny said, "That Colonel sure is a smart man. If he thinks what you are doing is important, I believe him."

"I believe him, too," said Sam.

CHAPTER 5

Sam Learns the Second Seed of Success

At the end of the work week, no one had lost a job at The Mercantile. On Saturday night, when most of the young men in town were out whooping it up, Sam found himself on the Colonel's back porch at Wilson Manor. The Colonel was there sipping a mint tea. "Let's review your week."

"I'm still employed," remarked Sam proudly.

"Well now, that's a surprise," teased the Colonel. They sat in silence for a time, enjoying the sunset as it faded over the banks of "Old Man River."

"Sam," the Colonel said.

"Yes, sir."

"My Grandpa Wilson was a generous man. He often brought me small gifts when he came to visit. One time when I was about five years old, he gave me a tin cup. I expected it to be filled with candy or a toy. Nope, it was full of dirt and had a couple of holes punched in the bottom.

"Well, you can imagine I wasn't all that excited about a cup full of dirt. So I asked him why he had given me a cup of dirt. He smiled, patted me on the head, and said it was much more than dirt. 'I want you to promise me you will pour a little water into that cup each day. Can you do that?' he asked.

"I shook my head yes, but after a couple of days, I started to forget to put water in my cup. Sometimes when I was in bed, I would remember. Then I would have to get up and go downstairs in the dark and cold. I started to get frustrated. I was irritated I ever made Grandpa that promise. The whole thing seemed like a waste of time.

"I watered that cup two weeks straight griping to myself most of the way. Then one morning I looked at my cup and there were two green sprouts in the middle of the dirt. They had not been there before. I was so excited! I ran to tell Grandpa. He listened quietly to my story and smiled. I told him that the water must be magic. He rubbed my head and said, 'It wasn't the water that was magic, it was your faithfulness.'

"You see, Sam, a small thing is a small thing, but a small thing done faithfully can become a great thing. You planted your first Seed of Success this week. It might seem like a small thing, but it is opening the door to a new and better life."

Hearing this made Sam feel good. In fact, he felt better and more hopeful than at anytime since he had had the conversation with his friend Dalton about the possibility of losing his job.

The Colonel sat back and crossed his legs. "Son, all of the Seeds of Success are important, but the second Seed has special significance. It not only will affect you at work but will impact in a positive way every aspect of your life, if you apply it consistently."

"What is this Seed?" asked Sam, unconsciously leaning forward.

The Colonel smiled and put his hand on Sam's knee. "Seed Number Two, 'Treat others as you wish to be treated.' " The Colonel then sat back and was silent.

Treat others as you wish to be treated.

Seed of Success
#2

Sam pondered the words, then repeated them, "Treat others as you wish to be treated.

"I think I've heard this before, Colonel, but I've never really thought about it. Is it an ancient principle too?"

"It is. A man named Jesus gave this advice over 2,000 years ago. It was great advice then, and it still works now. It works well because both life and work are about relationships. The better you are in your relationships, the better things will go for you at home, at work, with your friends, with your marriage...the list goes on and on.

"Close your eyes for a second." Sam did as he was instructed.

"Now imagine that every living person on the planet suddenly vanished and was gone. You are the only person left. You would inherit the land, gold, boats, buildings—everything! You would be the richest person that had ever lived. Are you picturing this, Sam?"

"Yes, sir," replied Sam.

"Wouldn't that be great? It would be all yours!"

After some thought Sam replied, "I reckon not."

"Well, why not?"

"I wouldn't have anyone to share it with," said Sam.

The Colonel smiled, "You just learned the secret to happiness. Life is all about people, and people are the real joy in life. You see, things were created to be used and people were created to be loved. But all too often we love things and use people.

This Seed of Success reminds us not to make that mistake. It's not stuff that makes us happy, it's our relationships and the people in them.

"If you want to be happy and effective at what you do, it's critical to develop good people skills. There is no substitute. The foundation for good people skills starts with treating others as you wish to be treated.

"Sam, in the coming week you are going to be faced with a person or situation that this Seed will apply to. When this happens, step back and ask yourself, 'How would I like to be treated?' and then respond that way."

Sam smiled as he thought about treating people like he would like to be treated. It just seemed like common sense. "I'll do it, Colonel, just like you say. Something just seems right about it."

"It seems right because it is right," said the Colonel.

CHAPTER 6

Sam Applies the Second Seed of Success

Sam was at work early Monday morning. As he walked up to The Mercantile from the back loading area, he was able to help a mule driver back his wagon up to the dock. "Thanks Sam," the seasoned old man said after the wagon came to a halt.

"You're welcome, sir—enjoy your day."

Sam put on his apron and started to set out tools for the men. Not only had Sam stayed late to clean up last week, but he also started to come in early to prepare things for the coming day.

Mr. Barney came in the warehouse with two cups of coffee. "I thought I might find you here." He handed Sam a cup of steaming coffee.

"Thank you, sir."

"Sam, I'm not sure what got into you last week, but I like it. Keep up the good work, son."

"Yes, sir," Sam said.

Dalton came in and saw Sam putting up the stock brought in by the mule team. Dalton adjusted his apron and then asked his friend, "Mr. Barney seems to have taken a shine to you. What did you do?"

Sam looked up from his work and said, "The Colonel has been helping me."

"Helping you how?" asked Dalton.

"He's been teaching me things to make me more valuable around here. Hopefully I'll become too valuable to be let go."

Dalton looked down and shuffled his feet. "Sam, will you teach me those things that will make me more valuable too?"

Sam's first thought was to keep the information about the Seeds of Success to himself. After all, if Dalton became more valuable, he might become competition for Sam if the job situation around The Mercantile really got rough. Sam looked at his friend, then asked himself how he would like to be treated if the situation were reversed.

Sam stood up, brushed his hands off on his apron, and reached out his hand. "You bet," he answered. "We'll start at lunch."

Sam got back to work unloading the wagon. While bending down to pick up a bag of oats he thought, "I just did seed number two." He smiled to himself, it felt good to help someone else, and he knew that his friendship with Dalton would strengthen because of it.

The call of his name brought him back. Mr. Barney was standing next to a tall man who had an appealing sense of strength about him. Somewhat younger than Mr. Barney, he was obviously a businessman, and a successful one at that.

"You called, sir?"

"Yes, Sam, please help Mr. Taylor out to his truck with this material." Mr. Taylor gave Sam a warm smile.

The man took a yellow calfskin wallet from inside his coat and paid his bill. "Thank you Mr. Barney, enjoy the rest of your day."

"I hope to see you soon, Mr. Taylor," said Mr. Barney. Mr. Taylor grabbed a crate and headed out the door. Sam followed with a box under each arm. When they were outside, Sam asked him, "Are you new in town, sir?"

"Why, yes I am," responded Mr. Taylor. "We just bought the old Preston place."

"That's a wonderful home," added Sam as they loaded the crates into the back of the truck.

Mr. Taylor shook Sam's hand and said, "I appreciate your help, Sam."

As he watched their customer drive off, he was impressed that Mr. Taylor had remembered his name. Sam turned to go back into The Mercantile when he noticed a yellow calfskin wallet on the ground. Sam reached down and picked up the wallet. The weight of it made him nervous. He imagined how the money stuffed inside it could help Granny and him through these tough times. Just then something flashed in his head—"Treat others as you wish to be treated." He knew what he must do. He placed the wallet deep in his worn overall pocket and went back to work. He picked up before he left, which was now becoming his usual routine. Then he headed to the Taylor home.

He stepped up on the wooden porch and knocked on the door. A pretty, dark-haired girl opened the door, "May I help you?" Sam just stood there staring into her dark magical eyes.

She was about to repeat her question when her father said, "Carly who's at the door?" Carly laughed, turned to her father and said, "I don't rightly know who it is, but I think a cat's got his tongue."

"Well, hello, Sam," said Mr. Taylor.

"Hello, sir," squeaked Sam.

"Sam, I'd like for you to meet my daughter." Carly held out her hand and smiled, sending Sam even deeper into a pit of infatuation. He thought she had the most beautiful smile he had ever seen. Her hand felt soft and good to touch.

Mr. Taylor broke the spell by asking Sam, "What can I do for you, son?" Sam finally regained his composure, reached into his pocket and pulled out Mr. Taylor's wallet. Mr. Taylor instinctively reached in his jacket pocket only to find it empty. "My heavens," he said.

Sam handed him the wallet and explained, "I found it in the street where your truck was parked. I recognized it from when you paid Mr. Barney."

Mr. Taylor checked the contents. "It's all there, sir. I didn't take a dime," said Sam. Mr. Taylor took Sam's hand and shook it vigorously.

"I'm sure it is, Sam. I was buying supplies for a large building job. There's a lot of money in there. I'm impressed you brought it back. A person could sure use this kind of cash during these hard times."

"Well, sir, it just seemed the right thing to do. I asked myself how I would like to be treated if I were in this situation. That's what brought me here."

"I see. Well, I think a reward is in order." Mr. Taylor started to reach inside his wallet for a bill.

"Oh no, sir. I just couldn't," said Sam.

Mr. Taylor sensed he shouldn't push the matter. "Thank you, Sam. It appears I have found a friend. He's about your age too, Carly."

Sam flushed bright red. He managed to wish them a good evening as he scurried off the porch making good his getaway.

Mr. Taylor put his arm around his daughter and said, "I think you bewitched that young man."

Carly hugged her dad back and said, "I feel a little bewitched myself."

CHAPTER 7

Sam's Good Deed Does Not Go Unrewarded

It was slow the next day at The Mercantile. Mr. Barney started sending workers home by noon. Sam and Dalton stayed busy, hoping to work as long as possible.

Sam felt a light punch on his arm and turned to see Dalton motioning to the front counter. "Check her out," said Dalton. Sam looked up and he felt his heart rate double. There stood Carly Taylor with her dad. Dalton saw the look on his face.

"Do you know her?" asked a surprised Dalton. Sam nodded. They saw Mr. Barney look in their direction. They both started to look very busy.

Sam heard Mr. Barney call his name and headed to the front counter. "Sam, I'm sure you remember Mr. Taylor. This is his lovely daughter, Carly."

Sam said, "Yes, sir, we met yesterday."

"Mr. Taylor told me what you did. It was quite honorable, young man."

"Thank you, sir."

"Mr. Taylor here is the state contractor for all building projects in this part of the county. He said he would like to start buying all his materials from The Mercantile—under one condition, that is...."

"Condition, sir?"

"Yes, that you personally handle his account. Looks like you just got promoted to account representative, son." Mr. Barney gleefully shook Sam's hand. Mr. Taylor shook Sam's hand also.

"Sam, in my position it is critical that I work with people I can trust. You passed that test yesterday. I'm sure we'll have a fine working relationship."

"I'll do my best, sir."

"Come by my office Monday and I'll give you your first order."

Sam watched as the Taylors left. He couldn't believe what had just happened. Mr. Barney came around the counter. He patted Sam on the back. "This account is very important to us. Everyone in the county has been after it since Mr. Taylor came to Natchez. You saved a lot of jobs today."

Mr. Barney had a crew meeting that afternoon. All the men seemed thrilled at the prospect of keeping their jobs. At the end of the meeting, Mr. Barney mentioned that Sam had gone out of his way for Mr. Taylor, and that's why they had this good fortune.

He told everyone it would be in his or her best interest to help Sam whenever he needed it in taking care of Mr. Taylor's account. Sam shifted in his spot as he felt all eyes on him. After the meeting, a large, older man in a faded blue work shirt came over to Sam and shook his hand. "I sure want to thank you for what you did. If you need anything, you come find Big Jim first."

Sam smiled and said, "You bet I will, Big Jim."

CHAPTER 8

Me, Myself, and I, Inc.

Sam couldn't get to Wilson Manor quick enough. "You will never guess what happened!" he blurted out as soon as he saw the Colonel.

A concerned Colonel looked at the out-of-breath young man and said, "Is it good news or bad news?"

"Good news. No, great news!"

"Slow down then and catch your breath and tell me about it. Here, let's sit under this magnolia tree." The Colonel sat down in the soft grass. Sam was too excited to sit. He began to recount the events of the past two days. The Colonel listened intently, clapping his hands at all the right times. When he finished, Sam fell to the grass in a heap.

The Colonel slapped him on the leg and said, "Good show, boy!" They sat for a while, enjoying the victory. Finally, the Colonel said, "I knew the Seeds of Success would work for you. I just didn't know you would see such great results so fast."

"Me neither. I think I've nailed Seed Number Two. Do you think we might move on early to Seed Number Three?"

The Colonel mulled this over for a minute, then said, "Sam, these Seeds of Success aren't points to be scored then forgotten. The Seeds must be planted, watered, and nurtured. You must take time to firmly establish these Seeds as daily habits so they become a part of you."

"Yes, sir," said Sam.

"You're right though, Sam. You appear to have nailed Seed Number Two, so let's celebrate. Mrs. Roosevelt made shoofly pie before she left. What do you say we have some and talk about Seed Number Three?"

Sam's adrenaline was flowing. He wolfed down his pie in a few delicious bites. He watched the Colonel leisurely savor every forkful of his pie. He was sure the Colonel was eating slowly just to tease him. He finally finished, gave a respectful belch, and then pushed back his plate.

"Sam, you see that back door? Hired a man once to do some painting for me. Took him all day to paint that door."

"Looks like he did a good job," said Sam.

"Yes, he did a good job. I fired him that same day."

"Fired him. I thought you said he did a good job."

"Well, by the time I bought the paint, then paid him to do the job, I could have bought a new door. You see, not every good job is a good investment. If he had finished his work in a few hours, like I thought he should have, it would have been a good deal for both of us. I would have had my door painted in a reasonable amount of time, and he would have gotten more work from me. As it stood, he was a bad buy."

"So he never worked for you again," asked Sam.

"He never worked for me in the first place," said the Colonel.

Sam looked confused. The Colonel, seeing he had boxed him into a corner, explained, "Sam, each and every one of us is our own boss. We are all the head of a company called 'Me, Myself, and I.' As head of that company, we trade or sell our products or services. In this man's case, he sold his painting skill.

"As far as I was concerned, I didn't want any more of what he was selling because I didn't feel that I was getting my money's worth. There wasn't enough value in his service."

"What could he have done to make his services more valuable to you," asked Sam.

"That's an excellent question, young man—it brings us to Seed Number Three, 'Work with a sense of urgency.' "

*Work with a
sense of urgency.*

Seed of Success
#3

"There's an old saying, 'Time is money.' There is a lot of truth in that statement, Sam, especially if you are the one paying for the time. Since most people trade their time for money, the way to excel is to make your time more valuable. You can do this in two ways: Get more done in the same amount of time, or do things that others can't or won't do. Most of the time it is hard to find work that others can't or won't do, so that leaves getting more done in the time allotted.

"You see, when you work with a sense of urgency you communicate to your employer that you understand the concept of time as money and show that you want to give excellent value for your employer's money. In this way, you not only make your employer feel that you are a good investment, but you also cause him or her to want to invest more in you."

"What if I work harder and faster, and I never see a raise?" asked Sam.

"Sam, there's always a shortage of great employees, even during a depression. Bosses are always watching for a sense of urgency in people, so if your boss doesn't appreciate that, another will. When you work with a sense of urgency, you automatically increase your value to the organization.

"Think of it this way, it's kind of like spreading fertilizer: You don't see results the instant you put it on; it takes some time. Yet the plant grows much faster and bigger and yields more fruit because of the fertilizer. A sense of urgency is your fertilizer. Start spreading it around. If you make it a habit every day, you will see your career grow faster. You will produce more fruit than you could ever imagine."

"So why don't we recap, Sam. Tell me the Seeds of Success that you've learned so far."

Sam said, "Well, sir, I learned to excel first so I can reap later. I must always do more on the job than is expected of me."

"Excellent," said the Colonel.

"Next, I should focus on the relationships in my life and strengthen them. I will do this by treating others as I wish to be treated."

"Very good," said the Colonel.

"This coming week, I will work with a sense of urgency so I can increase my value to my company and its customers."

The Colonel slapped Sam on the back and said, "You might be some decent help yet, boy!" They both laughed.

CHAPTER 9

Sam Delivers on Time

When Sam came to work on Monday morning, he was summoned to Mr. Barney's office. The office was simply furnished with a large, plain oak desk. Mr. Barney smiled and rose as Sam entered. "Well, today is your big day. Are you excited?"

"Yes, sir, excited and kind of nervous."

"Not to worry. Just keep doing the kind of job you've been doing and things will be great." Mr. Barney reached behind his desk and handed Sam a stack of clothes.

"Here's a little gift from your friends at The Mercantile." Sam stared at two pairs of pants, two white short-sleeved shirts, and a new pair of work shoes. Sam couldn't remember the last time he owned new store-bought clothes. All his stuff was hand-me-downs from family or friends.

Sam thanked Mr. Barney, as he was not sure what else to say. After changing, Sam felt somewhat uneasy in his new outfit. Although the clothes were stiff, they sure smelled better than his old overalls.

Sam went to the counter where Mr. Barney had just finished writing up an order for one of their regular customers. "Hello, Mrs. Jackson," said Sam.

"My Sam, don't you look smart today," she remarked. Sam blushed.

"Thank you, Ma'am."

Mr. Barney handed Sam the invoice. "This is Mrs. Jackson's order, Sam. She would like it delivered before the end of the day if possible." Sam smiled and nodded at Mrs. Jackson.

"I'll get right on it." After looking at the order, Sam decided Mrs. Jackson must be constructing a small building. He immediately started gathering the material with the help of Big Jim and a mule team. They unloaded the material at Mrs. Jackson's house by noon.

After a quick bite of lunch, Sam headed to Mr. Taylor's office for his first order. As he entered the office, Carly was coming out. Their eyes met and his brain stopped.

"Why, Mr. Sam, it certainly is a pleasure to see you here."

"Yes, ma'am," was all he could muster. She looked him over.

"You clean up right well, Sam." Sam desperately searched for something to say. He just could not get his brain to send words to his lips.

Carly came to his rescue. "I hear there's a carnival in town this weekend. Do you know anyone going?"

"Yes, ma'am, my friends and I go every year. It's a hoot. Would you like to come?" Sam couldn't believe the question came out of his mouth.

He was even more shocked when she said, "I'd love to! Pick me up at seven on Friday." She shook his hand and headed off to finish her shopping.

Sam was still shaken when he heard his name called. He looked up to see Mr. Taylor motioning him to his office. "Have a seat, Sam." After scanning the order Mr. Taylor handed him, Sam better understood why the account was so sought after.

"When do you need this by, sir?"

"Well today is Monday and my crew only has enough to do for one day without this order, so how about you have it to the job site by Wednesday morning?"

"Shouldn't be a problem, sir," said Sam. He knew it was a big order and that getting one that size ready usually took more than three days and there was only a day and a half until Wednesday morning, but he figured if he and a couple of other workers hustled they could get it there on time. Mr. Taylor and Sam shook hands. Sam hurried back to Mr. Barney with his prize order.

As Sam predicted, Mr. Taylor's order was filled and delivered by nine o'clock on Wednesday.

"Well done, Sam," said Mr. Taylor.

Sam literally ran back to The Mercantile with the cash payment from Mr. Taylor. He was scared to death having so much money in his pocket. Mr. Barney was extremely pleased to see the cash. He took out three dollars, handed it to Sam and said, "Here's a little bonus, Sam. Great job!"

Sam thanked him and grinned. He knew he would spend every dime on his date with Carly Taylor.

The rest of the week Sam focused on a sense of urgency. It seemed to be contagious with Dalton and Big Jim. They had become his constant companions. They were getting more work and deliveries done than ever before.

CHAPTER 10

Sam and Carly's First Date

The summer carnival was greatly anticipated by one and all in Natchez. Even with hard times and money scarce, people gathered for the fun and festivities.

With Mr. Taylor's blessing, Sam escorted Carly. They walked in silence until the air brought the wonderful aroma of cotton candy, corn dogs, and candy apples to their noses.

"I love candy apples," said an anxious Carly.

"I like everything," said Sam.

Most of the town was at the carnival and the atmosphere was quite festive. Their first stop was the candy apple stand, where they both sank their teeth into a large, delicious apple dipped in caramel. They found a bench and sat eating their treat while watching the crowd.

"I like to watch people," said Sam, in between bites. "I like to look at them and watch how they behave, try to figure out their story, you know."

Carly laughed and said, "Yeah, I do that too. What do you say we play a little game? Let's pick out people, and we'll each tell a story about them."

"I think I can do that," said Sam. They scanned the crowd looking for their first subject. Carly noticed a middle-aged man standing by the corn dog stand. He had his hands in his pockets and looked as if he might be anxiously waiting for someone.

"You see that man over there?" she asked, as she pointed in his direction. "He's waiting for someone," she started. "He's waiting on his girlfriend. He had to meet her here because long ago their fathers had a falling out, and even now after years have passed neither father would approve of their relationship. He desperately wants to see her. That's why he keeps shuffling his feet.

"When she finally arrives, they will go on a long walk and discuss their love for each other." Carly smiled and gestured that it was Sam's turn at the game.

"That sounds nice, but your Romeo and Juliet story is totally wrong."

She smiled and said, "Please correct me, Mr. Sam."

"I will. That man's name is Shifty Lewis. He's here to watch for potential victims for his pickpocket racket. His just spotted an elderly lady over there and plans to wait until she gets farther into the crowd, when he will sneak up to the helpless woman and relieve her of her fat, little pocketbook."

Sam seemed so convincing that Carly just looked at him and asked if he really knew this person. Sam looked her in the eye and said, "Certainly." He paused for dramatic effect.

Carly said, "We must go warn that poor woman."

Sam smiled and said, "I think she'll be okay. That's actually Elmo Jenkins. He's the barber in town. He always looks anxious like that."

Carly smiled and punched Sam on the arm. "You're too good at this, mister. Is he really the barber?"

"He sure is."

"He seems awful fidgety to be a barber."

"I said he was the barber. I didn't say he was a good barber." They both laughed.

"All right it's your turn to pick, Sam." He scanned the crowd and got a serious look on his face.

"Did you find someone?" asked Carly. Sam shook his head and stared at his feet. Carly noticed he had been looking at a young mother and her small son and daughter. "Do you know them?" she asked.

Sam nodded his head and said, "They live down the street from me. Her name is Kitty and the kids are Sharon and Tommy. She lost her husband the same time I lost my Ma. I know they don't have two nickels to rub together, so this must be hard on the kids to see all this and just be able to just look.

"Seeing them reminds me of my mom and sister." Sam went on to tell her about the loss he was feeling. When he was finished he was embarrassed about showing emotion in front of such a pretty girl. He rubbed his eyes and apologized.

"You don't need to apologize," she said matter-of-factly.

They sat, saying nothing for a while, until Carly asked, "Sam how much money were you planning on spending on our date tonight?"

Caught off guard by such a direct question, Sam said, "Well I reckon about three dollars. I got a bonus at work and wanted to make sure we had a real good time."

"That seems like a lot of money for just the two of us. I have two dollars myself. What do you say we pool our money and include Kitty and the kids tonight?"

Sam looked at her suspiciously and said, "I think what you're really saying is, 'Let's spend all of it on Kitty and the kids.'"

"Exactly," replied Carly.

Sam looked at her and said, "I really wanted to have a good time tonight with you, Carly. Will this spoil that?" She took his hand, kissed him on the cheek, and said, "On the contrary. I would really love to do this for them."

Sam smiled and said, "Let's go have some fun!"

Kitty was a little embarrassed about their offer but couldn't say no with the kids jumping up and down with excitement.

The evening was one of the best for the entire party, and no one wanted it to end. Sam and Carly walked Kitty home with little Sharon asleep in Sam's arms and a groggy Tommy not willing to leave Carly's side. They said "Good night," and Kitty hugged them both before going inside.

Carly and Sam walked slowly back to her house holding hands and saying nothing. Once at the door, she kissed him gently and said, "You're a fine person, Mr. Sam." And with that she went inside.

CHAPTER 11

Of Lieutenants and Solutions

The next week found the Colonel preparing for his yearly trip to New Orleans. He would take a steamer down the Mississippi reminiscing about days gone by. Once in New Orleans, he would walk the cobblestone streets of the French Quarter. He would eat French pastries at his favorite café, soaking in the sights and smells of this colorful section of the old city. There was something mysterious and compelling about the French Quarter.

As he packed, he thought about the history of New Orleans. He wondered if any of the previous generations had experienced the depths of hardship in which his dear country now found itself.

He promised himself he would discuss the next Seed of Success with Sam before leaving on his trip. He was fiercely proud of the young man. He knew Sam would apply this next Seed with the same vigor as the previous three.

Sam spent his week focusing on his sense of urgency. He found this actually made the job more fun. He loved the way people reacted when he exceeded their expectations.

He spent his evenings enjoying long walks along the river with Carly. This had been his regular schedule all week except for this Friday evening. Carly was attending a baby shower for a friend. Sam was grateful for the break only because this was the last night before the Colonel started his trip to New Orleans, and he hoped to learn the fourth Seed of Success before he left.

The Colonel and Sam sat for a while saying nothing, as only two friends comfortable with each other can. For his part, Sam waited patiently knowing the Colonel would reveal the next Seed in his own time. Finally, the Colonel said, "Sam, I'm very proud of you and the progress you are making. You've set a great foundation for your success at The Mercantile."

The Colonel continued, "During World War I, General Pershing found himself, along with his troops, trapped behind enemy lines. Reinforcements and supplies were cut off from them after an important bridge was destroyed. General Pershing stood at the edge of the river with a young lieutenant assessing the situation. The general told the lieutenant that this bridge was critical. It must be rebuilt. The general said Headquarters was working on a set of plans for the new bridge as they spoke. He told the lieutenant it was his job to complete the bridge once he had the plans in hand. The young lieutenant saluted the general and watched him drive off.

Two weeks had passed when the general sent the lieutenant a dispatch asking if the plans had arrived. The lieutenant sent a dispatch back saying they were still waiting on the plans, but the bridge was almost complete if he wished to use it."

Sam waited eagerly, wondering where the Colonel was going with the story. "Sam, when you're the owner or manager of a business, problems are constantly coming up. This constant barrage can sap one's strength—taking a heavy toll over time. When a boss feels bombarded with problems an opportunity is created for someone like yourself."

Sam asked, "Sir?"

"One man's problem is another man's opportunity," the Colonel replied. "That lieutenant seized the opportunity to solve the general's problem.

"This brings us to Seed Number Four, 'Be the solution, not the problem.' "

Be the solution,
not the problem.

Seed of Success
#4

"The first thing Seed Number Four addresses seems pretty obvious to most people, but you'd be surprised how many employees ignore it: Don't create problems.

"This can be as simple as showing up on time every day. Being at your station and ready to work when your shift starts. Not stretching your break past the time allotted for it. Not wasting your time and others' by chatting instead of working.

"But it also includes more important things like doing a good job on all the things your position calls for, even the things you like to do least and following all the company procedures, especially safety procedures.

"These are the relatively easy things that are expected of you, but you'd be surprised at how many people create problems by not doing them.

"But there's more to it. Let's step back now and try to look at things through Mr. Barney's eyes. Like we discussed, as a manager, he is under constant assault with problems and issues. What if, instead of going to Mr. Barney with problems that arise, someone started coming to him saying, 'Here's a problem but here's how I can solve it'? Wouldn't that be like a breath of fresh air for him? Don't you imagine Mr. Barney would be inclined to want to have this person around more, to give this person greater responsibility, and eventually to pay him or her more?

"Be a bright light for your boss, Sam. Start looking at challenging situations at work and figure out how to solve them. When your boss starts to think of you as the solution, you have taken one giant step.

Sam looked the Colonel in the eye and said, "I get it, 'Be a bright light' like you have been for me."

"Thank you, Sam, that means a lot to me," said the Colonel.

He left the next day for New Orleans, leaving Sam to figure out how to be the solution, not the problem.

CHAPTER 12

Sam Keeps on Trucking

Monday started with a flurry of activity at The Mercantile. Mr. Barney had Sam and Dalton scurrying all morning. As so often happens in business, it seemed everyone had decided to place their orders at the same time. Deliveries were headed to all ends of the county. For once, The Mercantile's delivery team was working at maximum capacity. On top of all this, John Meadows walked in. John was the contractor for the new schoolhouse expansion.

"Hello, Bill," said John as he approached the counter.

"Hi, John, what can I do for you?"

"Well, I'm in a big pinch today. I know those two by sixes were scheduled to be delivered Wednesday but my men finished the foundation sooner than I thought, and I need that material today."

Mr. Barney gave John a concerned look and said, "I'm sorry, John, but all our trucks and wagons are out for the day."

John looked frustrated. "If I don't get that material, my men won't be able to work today. I hate to do it, Bill, but I think I'll have to go over to Traders and see if they can get them to me today."

Sam, hearing the conversation from across the counter, approached the men. "Excuse me, sir, I'm not certain, but I think I might be able to get a truck if you'll excuse me for a while." Both men looked doubtful. Mr. Barney was about to say what he was thinking but then stopped. Sam was full of surprises lately. He decided to let him go. Mr. Barney smiled, motioned to the door, and said, "You most certainly can be excused."

Sam hustled out the door and headed for Mr. Taylor's office. Sam found him behind his desk. "Well hello, Sam."

"Hello, sir," said Sam catching his breath.

"What can I do for you, son?" Sam explained the situation with the schoolhouse and asked if he could borrow a truck for a little while. Mr. Taylor smiled at Sam and said, "I think we can spare one for such important work. Take the one out back."

The look on Mr. Barney's face was priceless. Before he could comment, Sam had the truck backed up to the dock and was giving loading instructions to Dalton and Big Jim. Mr. Barney and John Meadows watched from the door. When Sam walked by, John shook his hand and said, "Sam, I really appreciate this."

"Glad to be of service."

Once the truck was loaded, Sam and Big Jim left with the delivery. The men at the schoolhouse were thankful to see the material and willingly helped unload the truck. Like everyone else in the Delta, the men desperately needed the work.

Sam was pleased with himself as they headed back to return the truck. He felt he had been the solution to a problem. After a big thank you to Mr. Taylor, they walked back to The Mercantile. As they approached the store, Sam noticed an unusual number of people gathered on the front porch. Everyone seemed to be in deep conversation. As he got closer, Dalton spotted Sam and ran up to him. "Sam, have you heard?"

"Heard what?"

"It's about Mr. Barney. He fell from that ladder over there."

"How bad is he hurt?" Sam demanded.

"We don't know. He was unconscious when he left on a stretcher to the Doc's house."

Sam headed out the door and straight to the Doc's house two blocks away. He found Mrs. Barney in the waiting parlor. "Mrs. Barney, is Mr. Barney okay?"

She looked up at him and gave a faint smile. "The Doc said he has a bad concussion, a broken wrist, and a fractured ankle. He's pretty beat up, but he'll be okay with time." Sam waited with Mrs. Barney and some close friends until the Doc came out wiping his hands on a clean cloth.

Looking at the small group, he said, "He'll be fine as soon as the swelling goes down. He is going to need some bed rest and no activity."

Mrs. Barney went into the room to see for herself. She came out after a few minutes and motioned to Sam.

"He wants to see you, Sam." Sam found Mr. Barney lying in bed with a bandage around his head, his leg wrapped, and his arm in a sling. He looked up as Sam came in. "Hi, Sam."

"Hello, sir, I'm really glad you are going to be okay."

Mr. Barney nodded. "Sam, I haven't missed a day's work in twenty years. Now the Doc says I'm out for three to four weeks. That puts us in a real jam."

Sam walked over, grabbed his good hand, and patted it. "Not to worry, Mr. Barney. Mrs. Long does the bookwork. I know the sales and accounts now, and with Dalton in charge of deliveries, we'll be fine. We can hold down the fort until you are back in the saddle, sir."

Mr. Barney gave Sam's proposal some thought. "Maybe you're right, Sam. I'm going to need you to come by at close of business and report the day's events, but we'll give it a try.

Sam shook Mr. Barney's hand and said, "Consider it done."

CHAPTER 13

The Colonel Returns

For the next few weeks, Sam watched and supervised the activities at The Mercantile as if it were his own business.

Some of the other employees seemed a little sullen at first, but Sam remembered the Third Seed of Success and asked himself how he would like to be treated if he were them. He decided to treat them with the utmost respect, and when problems arose he went to them to ask their advice. Soon everyone was pulling as a well-formed team. Dalton and Big Jim were a big help.

Sam reported to Mr. Barney at the end of each day. Mr. Barney would nod his head in approval and give instructions on how things needed to be done. By the end of three weeks, the nods were beating the instructions ten to one. After a month had gone by, Mr. Barney was able to work half days. On the first day back, it took him quite a while to inspect the place, moving around slowly on his crutches, favoring his healing wrist and tender ankle.

When he finally finished his inspection, he sat on a stool by the counter and had all the staff come over. He told them how great the place looked and how proud he was of each and every one of them. As the others returned to work, Mr. Barney asked Sam to stay behind. He stressed how much he appreciated Sam's efforts. Sam said he was welcome, that he had been glad to help.

As Sam was about to leave, Mr. Barney asked, "By the way, Sam, how's that Carly girl doing?"

Sam blushed and said, "Okay I guess. Been working so much I haven't seen much of her for a while."

"That's what I thought, son. Why don't you take tomorrow off? It's Friday. I'll pay you for the full day. Go get caught up."

"Yes, sir," said Sam.

Friday was a great day for Sam. He and Carly spent the entire day at the local swimming hole. They shared a picnic lunch and just enjoyed being together.

The Colonel's schedule brought him back to town on the afternoon train. Sam planned to surprise him that evening with some of Granny's famous fried catfish.

Sam walked Carly home and gave her a couple of hours to get ready. The Colonel had met Carly but had not spent much time with her. Sam wanted his two friends to get to know each other.

The Colonel looked refreshed from his vacation and was ecstatic to see both of the young people. When he smelled Granny's catfish, he quickly led the small group to the kitchen. As they ate, Sam and Carly listened to the Colonel's step-by-step recounting of his journey.

The Colonel then asked Sam what was new at the store. With a wry smile, Sam said, "Glad you asked."

When Sam was through relating the events of the past month, the Colonel just shook his head. "Son, you never cease to amaze me."

Carly smiled at the Colonel and said, "Colonel, Sam's been telling me that you've helped him become more successful at The Mercantile. I would like to thank you."

The Colonel grinned and said, "No need to thank me, dear, Sam's like kin to me."

Finally, Sam brought up the subject he had so patiently waited for, "Colonel, it's been a month since I've seen you, and I think I've pretty well mastered Seed Number Four, 'Be the solution, not the problem.' Why don't we go over the fifth and final Seed?"

"I think that's a grand idea. The last Seed is both about pitching in when and where you're needed and about being humble. The Fifth Seed of Success is, 'Never say, "It's not my job." ' "

Never say,
"It's not my job."

Seed of Success
#5

"You won't confront this issue every day but when you do, remember, never say, 'It's not my job.' "

"Well, I think I can do that easy enough," said Sam, thinking that since he'd become Mr. Barney's right-hand man, the most arduous and menial jobs were done by other employees at The Mercantile. The only things he was asked to do now were things he thought of as more important, and he was happy to do them.

As Sam and Carly walked home hand-in-hand, they discussed Seed Number Five.

"That one doesn't seem very applicable to me," said Sam.

"Well, I'd do what the Colonel says. He's a remarkable man," commented Carly.

"You're right. I just don't think I'll ever use it."

Little did Sam know.

CHAPTER 14

Sunday Lunch

That Sunday, Mr. Taylor invited Sam to the Belmont Hotel for Sunday lunch. Sam had never been to a fancy sit-down restaurant before. The Belmont was an overwhelming ten stories tall. He had taken the elevator all the way to the top once with his Ma. They had stood on the roof and admired the view. It was one of the highlights of his young life.

Sam arrived at the hotel a little early. He had borrowed a suit from his cousin Tyrell that was too large for him. It felt stiff and unfamiliar. As he approached the hotel's front entrance, he ran his finger along one of the smoothly carved marble railings that flanked the door. He felt strange in a place of such elegance. He noticed the bell captain's uniform looked a lot like his cousin's borrowed suit.

He was about to sit down on the lobby sofa and wait when a plump, red-faced little man came in from the side door. He was dragging a heavy, over-stuffed bag. He saw Sam standing there and said, "Thank goodness, you can carry this to my room for me, young man." Sam almost said, "I don't work here," Then he remembered the Fifth Seed. Telling the man he didn't work here would be the same as saying, "It's not my job."

Sam looked at the winded man and said, "No problem, sir," and picked up the bag. They took the elevator to the eighth floor and got out.

The man finally got his breath back and asked Sam, "Do you know where The Mercantile is?"

Sam smiled and said, "Yes sir, that's where I work."

"Oh, do you work here at the hotel on the weekends then?"

"No, sir, I'm here to meet my girlfriend's family for lunch."

The little man looked confused. "Well, if you don't work here why are you carrying my luggage?"

"Because you asked me, and you looked like you could use the help," said Sam. When they reached the man's room, he tried to tip Sam. Sam cheerfully refused and told the man he was glad he could be of help. The grateful man introduced himself as Ronnie Greer.

"Pleased to meet you, Mr. Greer. The Mercantile is right at the end of the street. It would be a pleasure to serve you. I'll help anyway I can."

 CHAPTER 15

Sam Takes the Fall

Life on Monday seemed almost back to normal. Mr. Barney was perched on a stool at the front counter. He was glad to be at work and out of the house.

About noon, Abigail Watkins' farmhand, Charlie, came in and asked if they had any more of a certain kind of barbed wire. Charlie needed it to repair a fence one of Mrs. Watkins' cows had knocked down. "I've looked all over," Charlie said, "but no one seems to have any of that kind left."

About that time, Sam was passing by the counter. Mr. Barney asked him to go up into the attic where he thought a roll of barbed wire might still be stashed. The attic was hot and dusty, and Sam was a bit offended that Mr. Barney would expect him to go digging around up there. He almost suggested Mr. Barney send Big Jim to do it when he remembered the Fifth Seed of Success, "Never say, 'It's not my job.' "

"I'll look right now," Sam said.

Access to the attic was through a hinged door in the ceiling. You pulled a rope and the door opened and a wooden ladder unfolded. Sam headed up the rickety ladder into the attic, knocking down cobwebs as he went. Dust covered the old wood floor. Apparently no one had been up here in ages.

Sam's search seemed destined to be in vain when he spotted what might have been a roll of the wire on a shelf beneath some empty boxes. When he pulled on the roll, the boxes tumbled down on him covering him in dust.

Sam had begun to sweat in the attic's heat, so when he tried to wipe the dust from his arms and face, it just turned into a kind of gray, gritty mud. "Great," thought Sam. But at least it was a roll of the wire Charlie was after.

Sam hoisted the wire onto his shoulder and headed for the ladder. He hadn't taken two steps when the old floor beneath him made a groaning noise and broke away. Sam fell through The Mercantile's ceiling in a cloud of dust. For a moment he thought he might be injured, but luckily a pile of sacks of winter grain broke his fall. He sat up on the sacks and looked around to find that everyone in the building was staring at him. When they realized he hadn't been hurt, they all broke out laughing.

Sam pictured what a comic sight he must be, sitting on grain sacks covered in dust, and started laughing too.

Big Jim came over and helped Sam off the pile of sacks. Sam looked at Big Jim and realized he was glad Big Jim hadn't been sent into the attic. The bigger, older man might have been hurt in the fall. Sam silently thanked the Colonel for teaching him the Fifth Seed of Success. "Funny how things work out when you practice the Seeds," he thought.

Just then, Sam heard his name called from the far side of the store. He was pleasantly surprised to see Mr. Greer coming over with Mr. Barney. They both had big smiles on their faces. Apparently they had witnessed his fall too.

"Hello, Mr. Greer," Sam said sheepishly. "I hope you got settled in okay, sir."

Shaking Sam's hand he said, "Thanks to you I did, Sam."

"Sam, Mr. Greer works for the South Central Railroad. He is in charge of a large building project. He's in the area shopping for a good supplier. You know anyone who fits that bill?" smiled Mr. Barney.

Sam looked at Mr. Greer and said, "Sir, we would love to be that supplier. We'll work hard to meet all your needs."

"You know, Sam, I think any company that would employ a fellow like you must be a good one. I'll give it a try." Mr. Greer shook Sam's hand again.

After Mr. Greer left, Mr. Barney looked at Sam and just shook his head. Sam asked, "Are you okay, sir?"

"You're remarkable, Sam. You always seem to be at the right place at the right time."

Sam smiled and said, "I've had an outstanding teacher."

CHAPTER 16

A Thanksgiving Surprise

Sam spent the rest of the summer planting his seeds and teaching everyone around him how to plant their own seeds of success. He found he enjoyed helping others become better at their jobs.

By fall, The Mercantile had grown so much they needed to expand. As the holidays were approaching, Sam found himself very excited about this year's Thanksgiving.

He and Granny were having dinner at the Taylor home. The Taylors had invited the Colonel, Mr. and Mrs. Barney, and some of the

Taylors' new neighbors. Sam knew it would be a feast to remember.

The cool, autumn air reached even Natchez this year. It felt good after the long, hot summer. As Sam had anticipated, the meal was the best he had ever had. Everyone ate until they were stuffed. When the meal was complete, Mr. Taylor tapped his fork on his glass to get everyone's attention at the large table. Once everyone became silent he said, "Thank you all for coming today. It truly has been a wonderful year and I thank you all for being a part of it. Now, I believe Mr. Barney has something to say."

Mr. Barney stood with ease. His ankle had completely healed. He paused, cleared his throat, and then spoke. "We have been blessed this year at The Mercantile beyond our wildest dreams. Our sales and profits have doubled and all of this during the worst depression our dear country has ever experienced.

"We now find ourselves in a very interesting position. We must expand to accommodate all this new business. I've approached my friends, the Colonel and Mr. Taylor here, to help form a new partnership to make this growth possible. To my great pleasure they accepted."

All at the table clapped. Then Mr. Barney held up his hand for silence. "We still lack the last piece of the partnership—a fourth person. A person who will work hard and smart to help secure the future of The Mercantile. We three partners unanimously agree that the fourth partner should be Sam."

All eyes went to Sam. He just sat there frozen. Mr. Barney continued, "Sam, much, if not most, of our new growth is coming because of you and the now famous Seeds of Success. You have unselfishly shared them with your fellow workers. Consequently, you have helped put us in the position we currently enjoy. What do you say, Sam?"

I don't know what to say," he replied.

"Just say yes," said the Colonel.

They all laughed and Sam said, "I'd be honored!" The entire table clapped and cheered. When the celebration quieted down, Sam stood and said, "I'd like to say something if it's all right."

Mr. Taylor nodded and said, "By all means speak up."

Sam, searching for the right words, finally began, "This last year I thought I would never be happy again. After Mama and Rachael passed, I went into a pit of deep despair. Only by the grace of God and the support of Granny and the Colonel did I make it through that time. I'd like to thank you both."

Granny smiled between sniffles.

Sam continued, "It was then that the Colonel started to share the Seeds of Success with me. He promised I wouldn't be disappointed if I learned to use them, but never did I imagine all of this. The Colonel taught me that you reap what you sow. If you want to reap good rewards, you must plant good seeds. Planting these seeds changed my life.

The Colonel also taught me that success and happiness are based on relationships, not on things. This knowledge is a gift in itself, and I thank you for it."

It was now the Colonel's turn to dab his eyes as he stood and hugged Sam. Standing beside the Colonel, Sam continued, "Thank you, Mr. Barney, for this wonderful opportunity."

"You're absolutely welcome, Sam! Just think. Now you will have enough money to afford a wife and family."

Blushing, Sam and Carly looked at each other. Sam took her hand and tenderly kissed it. Carly smiled the beautiful smile Sam had noticed the first day he met her.

"I think that means 'yes,' " said the Colonel. He then raised his glass and gave a toast to Carly and Sam.

"May they live happily ever after!"

The Five
Seeds of Success

Excel first, reap later.

*Treat others as you
wish to be treated.*

*Work with a
sense of urgency.*

*Be the solution,
not the problem.*

*Never say,
"It's not my job."*

Help others to benefit from the five Seeds of
Sucess. Share this book with a friend or coworker.

ABOUT THE AUTHOR

During a very difficult, low point in his business career, Jack Myrick found himself looking at those working with him and blaming them for his circumstances. He thought, "If they would just do their jobs like they were supposed to, then I wouldn't be in this situation."

At the end of his rope, Jack took some time off for reflection. By stepping back and looking at his situation he realized he had two choices: either quit and find a new career or change. By being totally honest with himself, he discovered that before his circumstances could change, he had to change.

Jack began to ask himself, "What kind of leader could turn this situation around?" Eventually he developed some simple leadership principles, as well as strategies on how to implement them. The effect was so dramatic for him, he knew he had to share them with others so he wrote his first book, *The Shipbuilder*.

Jack then turned his attention to helping people excel at their jobs. The result is his second book, *The Merchant.*

The five seeds of success outlined in *The Merchant* work because they focus on getting the job done. They smooth the sometimes bumpy road to advancement. And they help us connect with and assist our coworkers—to our benefit and theirs. Apply the seeds starting today and you to will discover a wonderful transformation.

Jack Myrick is president and founder of Management Solutions, a management training company, as well as head of Myrick Enterprises, a restaurant development group. He lives in Central Oklahoma and is blessed with a wonderful wife and three incredible daughters.

You can contact Jack Myrick at
jack@publicstrategies.com.

Speakers—Experience an inspiring and powerful program that presents *The Shipbuilder* or *The Merchant* principles and offers strategies on how to apply them.

Workshops—Bring the skills for change directly to your people. These in-depth trainings are fun, informative, four-hour workshops based on the five leadership principles of *The Shipbuilder* or the five seeds of success of *The Merchant.* Each workshop attendee receives a hardcover copy of *The Shipbuilder* or *The Merchant,* a workbook, and a lifetime's worth of career tools.

Jack Myrick's presentations and workshops are known for their Southern charm and practicality.

For information, please call
405-848-2171
or e-mail jack@publicstrategies.com